NELSON SCIENCE

Properties of Matter

Ted Gibb

 I⟨T⟩P® Nelson

an International Thomson Publishing company

Toronto • Albany • Bonn • Boston • Cincinnati • Detroit • London • Madrid • Melbourne •
Mexico City • New York • Pacific Grove • Paris • San Francisco • Singapore • Tokyo • Washington

Contents

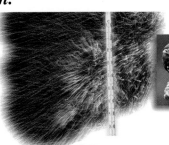

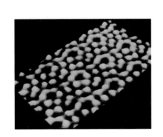

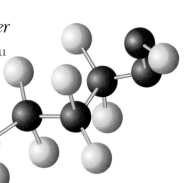

A chance to use problem-solving skills

 Important safety information

 Record observations or data

 Design or build

 A challenge

 Work together

 Wash hands with soap and water

What is Matter?

WHAT DO YOU SEE WHEN you look around? Matter. Everything you see, touch, taste or smell is matter. Matter is the name given to all the substance in the universe. It even includes the air you breathe. In fact, the variety of matter appears to be endless.

To say that matter is substance is not really enough, though. Exactly what is matter? **Matter** is anything that has mass and occupies space (has volume).

What is matter made of? This is a more difficult question, because the building blocks that make up matter cannot be observed directly. We must rely on a model, or mental picture, that has been created based on many observations of matter and the changes that matter undergoes.

In this unit, you will learn to accurately describe matter in its variety of forms. You will discover through investigation that the characteristics of a substance often determine how it is used. Finally, you will examine how matter changes.

The closer you look at matter, the more interesting it gets. Even smoothly polished metal, like the cog below, shows some bumps if you magnify it enough (left).

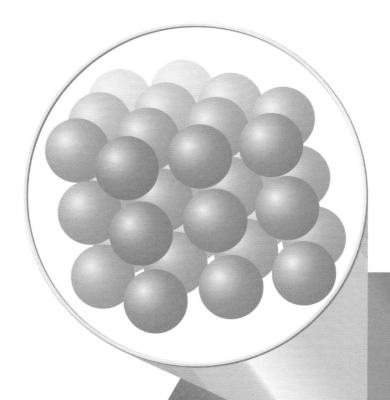

What is matter made of? What would metal, marble, or malted milk look like if you could magnify it enough? Perhaps metal would look like this–stacks of very tiny particles.

1. Carefully examine the photograph of the cog.

   a) How would you describe the cog to a friend who has not seen the photograph?

   b) Do you think wood could have been used for the cog? Why or why not?

2. Each of the four musical instruments below represents a category or family of instruments. Examine the instruments.

   a) What makes each instrument different from the others?

   b) Which family of instruments would a piano belong to? Justify your choice.

Journal Entry

3. Matter is changing all around us. Some of the changes are small — for example, when you pluck a guitar string, and it produces a musical note. Some changes are more dramatic — leaves changing colour in the fall, or gasoline burning in an engine. Record in your journal any changes in matter you see as you go about your daily activities.

Observing Properties

WHEN YOU SAY A DISH looks good, smells delicious, feels gooey, and tastes great, you are using your senses to observe the food you are eating. What you are describing are the characteristics, or **properties**, of the food.

In this investigation, you will use your senses to observe the properties of a variety of materials.

Substances have many properties. For example, what do you think each of the substances on the right feels like? How objects feel, a property called **texture**, helps us tell the difference between them.

Materials

- safety goggles
- apron
- samples of different substances
- spoon or tweezers
- containers with water

Procedure

1 Copy the following table into your notebook.

Substance	State (solid liquid, or gas)	Colour	Living or Nonliving	Texture (what it feels like)	Solubility (how well it mixes with water)

2 Examine each substance in its container.

a) Which of your senses did you use to make your observation?

b) Record in your table a description of each substance's state, colour, and whether it is living or nonliving.

3 Use the spoon or tweezers to remove a small amount of each substance from its container.
- Observe its texture.

c) Which of your senses did you use to make your observation?

d) Record your observations.

4 Place each of the samples you removed earlier into a container half filled with water.

■ Cover the container and shake. If the water and the sample form a single clear liquid, the sample has dissolved.

e) Record which of the substances dissolve.

Investigation Questions

1. **a)** Name three properties of a substance that you can observe using your sense of sight.

    b) Name two properties that you can observe using any of your other senses.

Extension

2. Make a list of eight objects in your classroom and describe each object.

3. Organize 10 snack foods into groups by properties. Describe the properties on which you based your classification.

4. Can you think of two additional properties that could be tested using the substances in this investigation? Devise a method to determine these properties. With the approval of your teacher, carry out your investigations.

Properties of Matter

YOU USE PROPERTIES to describe and identify matter, and to predict how it will behave. Each property you study helps to identify matter more completely. Early scientists studying matter began to group materials by common properties. Through careful observations, much information about a variety of substances was obtained.

Today, substances are usually first described by the property of state. Is the substance a solid, a liquid, or a gas? Additional properties, such as colour, texture, odour, taste, lustre, and clarity can all be observed using only your senses. Other properties, such as **solubility** (how well a substance dissolves in another substance), **strength** (resistance to breaking), **elasticity** (ability to return to the original form after stretching), **viscosity** (how easily a liquid pours), and **hardness** may require tests or measurements to describe.

State

All substances can be classified as solid, liquid, or gas. The roller blades are solid. Water is a liquid. Air is a gas.

Colour

This leaf appears green because it reflects green light back to your eyes. All objects that appear green reflect green light.

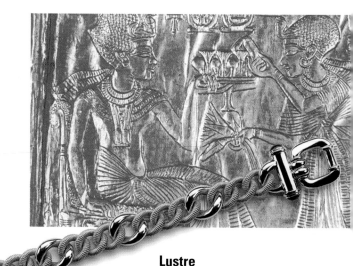

Lustre

Most metals, such as gold, copper, and silver, have lustre — they appear shiny.

Clarity

Clarity ranges from transparent to opaque. Glass is transparent (or clear)—it allows light to pass through. The window frame is opaque—it does not allow light to pass through.

Properties Requiring Simple Tests or Measurements

Conductivity

Electricity flows through metal (usually copper or aluminum) wires. These metals are described as good conductors. On the other hand, the plastic covering prevents electricity from leaving the wire. Plastic is a poor conductor (also called an insulator).

Malleability

A solid that can easily be hammered into any shape is said to be malleable. Gold and other metals tend to be malleable, but clay pottery is not malleable. Clay is brittle. It breaks easily when hit with a hammer.

Ductility

A solid is ductile if it can be pulled into wires.

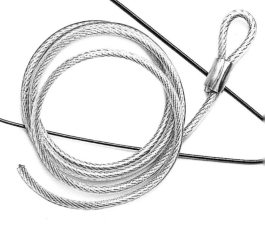

SELF CHECK

1. Name the three states of matter and give one example of each.

2. **a)** List four properties that you can observe using only your senses.

   b) Name four properties that require simple tests or measurements to describe.

Apply

3. For each of the properties you named in 2 b), describe a simple test or measurement you might perform.

Extension

4. Hardness is the resistance of one substance to being scratched or dented by another. Obtain samples of a variety of substances. Scratch one against the other to determine their relative hardness. Order the samples from the hardest to the softest.

5. Mineralogist Friedrich Mohs developed a system to order minerals according to their hardness. Research the Mohs scale and the hardness of different minerals.

Survival

Y OU HAVE LEARNED THAT you can use your senses to make observations about the properties of a substance. Now, how are those properties useful? The **function** or application of an object is how it is used. Function depends on the properties of the substances that make up the object. But a substance can have many different functions. For example, diamonds are so hard that they can be used to cut through rock. But diamonds are also valuable as jewellery because of their colour and lustre. The properties of a substance are always the same, but the function of a substance can change.

Your group has survived a plane crash. You have salvaged some items from the wreck, and now you must decide if the items are important enough to keep. How important is each item? You will have to carefully examine the properties of each item to be sure.

Procedure

1 First, you must identify each of the items you have salvaged. In your group, identify each item by matching it with one of the descriptions in the Properties of Salvaged Items list.

a) Record which item matches each description.

Properties of Salvaged Items

1. Solid, black, smooth, cylindrical, with a clear, colourless bulb at one end

2. Solid, rectangular, very thin, flexible, covered with lines and symbols, can be folded

3. Solid, metallic, folds in half, very sharp

4. Solid, flexible, waterproof, very thin, large size

5. Solid, white, porous, absorbent, about 5 cm square

6. Small bottle containing white objects that dissolve in water and that melt ice

7. 6 L of a liquid that has no odour, is clear, colourless, and tasteless

8. Solid made of many small, thin sheets held together with a sticky substance; each of the thin sheets is covered with marks

9. Bent wire holding two clear, dark glass lenses

10. 1-L plastic bottle containing a clear, dark liquid that has a sweet taste

11. Flat, rectangular solid with one silver reflective surface; breaks easily

12. Cylindrical solid with a movable, magnetic arm

Investigation Questions

1. Was it difficult to decide what some of the objects were using only the descriptions provided? Which ones, and why?

2. Were the functions you listed for the items the same as those listed by other members of your group? Why, or why not?

3. What is the difference between an observation and a function or application?

4. How did the properties of each item relate to its functions?

Extension

5. Choose two items and improve the description of their properties. For example, would measurements help to describe an item more accurately?

6. Should function be included in the description of an object? Explain why or why not.

2 Before you can decide which items are most important, you must know what you can use them for. What are the functions of each item?

b) On your own, list as many functions as you can for each item.

3 Now your group can rank each item according to its importance for survival, starting with the most important item. Remember: your survival as a group at the crash site depends on how well you share your knowledge and talents!

Be prepared to defend your group's ranking.

c) Create a list ranking each of the items that have been salvaged, with the most important item first.

Quantitative and Qualitative Properties

WHEN YOU DESCRIBE properties such as colour, shape, and texture that you have observed using your senses, these properties are said to be qualitative. **Qualitative** properties are ones that are not measured.

When you count the number of pencils in a package and use the number to describe the package, the observation is said to be **quantitative**. Quantitative properties are ones that are measured.

Taking Measure

Any measurement is a quantitative observation. Most of the countries in the world now use the Système International (SI) for standard units of measurement. These units are based on powers of 10 and are therefore easy to use in calculations.

The basic SI unit for mass is the **kilogram** (kg). The mass of large objects, such as cars, is measured in kilograms. The mass of small objects, such as a package of pasta, is measured in grams. A gram (g) is 1/1000 of a kilogram. Still smaller objects, such as a piece of pasta, are measured in milligrams. A milligram (mg) is 1/1000 of a gram.

The **litre** (L) is the basic SI unit for volume. Gasoline is measured in litres. Smaller volumes, such as the volume of pop in a can, are measured in millilitres. One millilitre (mL) is 1/1000 of a litre. Volume can also be measured in cubic metres (1 m^3 = 1 m wide × 1 m high × 1 m deep). A cubic metre is equal to 1000 L. The amount of concrete needed to pour the foundation of a house would be measured in cubic metres.

Mass is a property shared by all substances. It describes the amount of matter in a substance. It is a quantitative property that can be easily measured using a balance.

Volume is another quantitative property shared by all matter. Measuring the amount of water required to fill a container will give you the volume of the container. You can also calculate the volume of regular objects by measuring their length, width, and height.

Pizza Properties

Quantitative Properties	Quantitative Observations
Mass of pizza	402 g
Volume of pizza dough	103 cm³
Number of slices	8
Mass of pepperoni	37 g
Qualitative Properties	**Qualitative Observations**
Colour of pizza	mostly pale yellow with circular red pieces; also some green, black, and brown pieces
Taste of pizza	great!, but a little salty

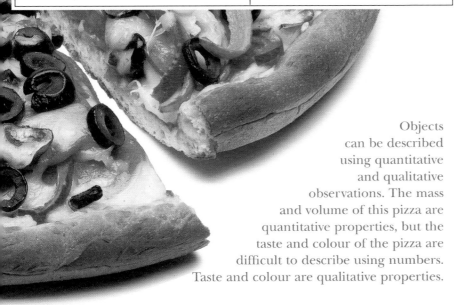

Objects can be described using quantitative and qualitative observations. The mass and volume of this pizza are quantitative properties, but the taste and colour of the pizza are difficult to describe using numbers. Taste and colour are qualitative properties.

TRY THIS

What Am I?

In your group, write a description of a common object (e.g., a toothbrush) on a filing card, using both qualitative and quantitative observations. Do not include functions, and do not draw the object. Exchange cards with another group. Can the other group identify your group's object from the description on the card?

• Ask the other group to add information to the card that would have helped in identifying your object.

• Would a life form from another galaxy know what your object was? What more might it need to know about the object?

SELF CHECK

1. Explain in your own words the meaning of each of the following terms:
   a) property
   b) function or application
   c) qualitative property
   d) quantitative property

2. Classify each of the following observations as either qualitative or quantitative.
   a) The bottle holds six litres.
   b) This liquid is clear and colourless.
   c) This liquid is flammable.
   d) Water boils at 100°C.
   e) These skis are 180 cm long.
   f) This gas is colourless and tasteless.

3. Write one qualitative and one quantitative observation to describe each of the following.
   a) yourself
   b) a sport drink
   c) a cola drink
   d) your favourite snack food
   e) your level of performance in your favourite subject

4. Label each of the observations below as qualitative or quantitative. Where an observation is qualitative, replace it with one that is quantitative.
   a) The hockey player was overweight at the start of training camp.
   b) A 500-mL container of honey costs $2.99.
   c) Joan scored better on her math test than Emile did.
   d) Donovan is the world's fastest human.

5. What unit of measurement would be appropriate to measure each of the following?
   a) the volume of air in your classroom
   b) the volume of a can of beans
   c) your body mass
   d) the mass of a peanut shell
   e) the mass of a bag of peanuts

Measuring Mass

MANY EVERYDAY PRODUCTS, including meat, sugar, and some dairy products, are purchased by the gram or kilogram. These are units of mass, the measure of the amount of matter in a substance.

In this investigation, you will design equipment to measure mass. You will also use your classroom balance to measure the mass of a liquid.

Materials

- apron
- pencil
- Plasticine
- beakers or containers
- board
- variety of small objects
- metal nuts or bolts
- mass balance
- liquid sample

Like a teeter-totter, a mass balance comes to the horizontal position when equal masses are the same distance from the balance point.

Procedure

Part 1: A Homemade Balance

1 Examine the picture of the homemade balance.
  ■ Make your own homemade balance using the materials provided by your teacher and using the photograph as a guide.

2 Adjust the balance until it is horizontal.
  ■ Place an object on one side of your homemade balance.
  ■ Add nuts or bolts on the other side until your balance returns to the horizontal position.
  ■ Repeat using other objects, one at a time.

a) What happens to the balance when an object is placed on one side?

b) How were you able to return the balance to the horizontal position?

c) Record the mass of each object. What "units" did you use?

Investigation Questions

1. Why is it important to have a balance leveled before you make any measurements?

2. In step 3, your group took several measurements and found the average. Why is this an advisable procedure?

3. How could you have improved the procedure in Part 2?

Apply

4. To measure the liquid sample in Part 2, you used "indirect measurement." Explain what is meant by indirect measurement.

Extension

5. Design a homemade balance that you think would be more accurate than the one you constructed. Explain why your design is an improvement.

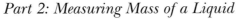

Part 2: Measuring Mass of a Liquid

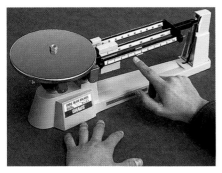

3 Use your classroom balance to determine the mass of a nut. Each student in your group should take a turn at finding the mass.

d) Calculate the average mass of a nut.

e) From the average nut mass, calculate the mass in grams of each object you measured on your homemade balance.

4 Use your classroom balance to find the mass of a clean, dry beaker.

f) Record your measurement.

g) Why is it important that the beaker be dry?

5 Pour the sample of liquid into the beaker.
  ■ Measure the mass of the beaker and the liquid sample.

h) Record the combined mass.

i) Calculate the mass of the liquid sample.

Measuring Volume

HOW MANY CONTAINERS CAN you stack in the hold of a ship? The answer depends on the space each container takes up, and the space available in the ship (the volume of the ship). Volume can be thought of as the amount of space inside something that is hollow, or as the space occupied by something.

To calculate the volume of a rectangular container, you first measure the length, width, and height of the box. Then you multiply the three measurements to obtain the volume.

$$\text{Volume} = \text{length} \times \text{width} \times \text{height}$$

But not all objects are rectangular. How would you find the volume of a stone? In this investigation, you will measure the volume of liquids and small, irregular solids.

Materials

- apron
- unmarked clear cylindrical container
- ruler
- blank white paper
- black permanent marker
- sample volume of liquid
- graduated cylinder
- variety of small, irregular solids

Procedure

Part 1: Volume of a Liquid

1 Make a mark on the side of the cylindrical container close to the top. This will represent a 1-container volume.

■ Use the ruler to make marks along the side of the container to represent other volumes. For example, place a mark equidistant between the top and bottom to represent a 1/2 or 0.5-container volume.

2 Use your volume measure to find the volume of a sample of liquid.

a) Record the volume of the liquid. What unit of measurement did you use?

b) Did you have any difficulty finding the volume of the sample?

c) Was your measurement of volume the same as those of other groups? Why or why not?

3 Pour the liquid sample into a graduated cylinder. Use the graduated cylinder to find the volume of the liquid.

d) Record the volume of the liquid sample. What units did you use?

e) Why is it helpful to hold a piece of white paper behind the graduated cylinder when reading the volume?

Part 2: Volume of Irregular Solids

4 Pour about 10 mL of water into a graduated cylinder and read the volume.

🖉 f) Record the volume in your notebook.

5 Tilt the graduated cylinder and gently slide a small object into the water.
  ■ Measure the volume of the water and the object.

🖉 g) Record the volume of the water with the object in it.

🖉 h) Calculate the volume of the object. Use the following equation.

Volume of object = volume of water with object – volume of water

Investigation Questions

1. In Part 2, you used the displacement of water to measure the volume of an irregular solid.
   a) Explain why "displacement of water" is an appropriate term for this method.
   b) Why is this an indirect measurement?

2. When would the displacement of water not be a good method for finding the volume of an irregular object?

Apply

3. Describe two everyday situations in which the measurement of volume is important.

4. This bolt and piece of chalk are nearly the same length and thickness (volume). What properties could you use to identify these two substances?

Extension

5. Are the following statements correct? Explain.
   a) A piece of Plasticine has a larger volume when pressed flat than when it is rolled into a ball.
   b) No two objects can occupy the same space at the same time.
   c) The volume of your thumb can be measured by immersing it in a known volume of water.

6. Compare packages of products purchased at a supermarket. Measure the mass and volume of the contents of each package and compare them with the mass and volume printed on the package. How do the measured and advertised values compare?

Comparing Volume and Mass

The mass of the metal cube and the mass of water that fills the jug are equal. What difference do you notice?

YOU KNOW THAT MASS and volume are important properties of matter. You have measured the mass and volume of different substances using a variety of equipment and methods. But there is still a question about mass and volume that remains: how are mass and volume related?

Materials

- apron
- balance
- graduated cylinder
- water
- graph paper

Procedure

1 Create a data table in your notebook like the one below.

Mass of graduated cylinder (g)	Volume of water sample (mL)	Mass of graduated cylinder and water sample (g)	Mass of water sample (g)

2 Measure the mass of a dry, empty graduated cylinder using a balance.

a) Record the mass of the empty cylinder in your table.

3 Pour 10 mL of water into the graduated cylinder.
■ Measure the mass of the water and graduated cylinder.

b) Record the mass of 10 mL of water and the cylinder.

c) Calculate the mass of 10 mL of water and record it.

The volume of the metal cube and the volume of the water in the jug are equal. What difference do you notice?

4 Add another 10 mL of water to the graduated cylinder. Measure the mass of the 20 mL of water and the cylinder.

✎ d) Record the total mass in your table.

✎ e) Calculate the mass of 20 mL of water and record it in your table.

5 Repeat step 4 to measure the mass of 30, 40, and 50 mL of water.

✎ f) Record all your measurements and calculations in your table.

Viscosity, a Property of Liquids

YOU HAVE STUDIED PROPERTIES that all matter has — mass and volume. But some properties describe only one state of matter. Consider liquids, for example. Not all liquids are the same. Every liquid has its own "thickness" or viscosity. Some liquids, such as milk or water, pour quickly. They have a low viscosity. Others, such as syrup or honey, pour slowly. They have a high viscosity. **Viscosity** is a property of liquids that describes the way they pour.

You can think of viscosity as a measure of resistance to movement. All liquids will slow an object falling through them. The greater the viscosity of the liquid, the more slowly an object will fall through the liquid.

Materials

- apron
- goggles
- 500–750 mL clear plastic containers with water, cooking oil, shampoo, and honey

- black permanent marker
- marbles or other small spherical objects
- stopwatch or other suitable timing device

Procedure

1 Make a table to record your data.
  ■ Choose one of the four liquids.
  ■ On the side of a container, place two black marks, one near the top and the other about 2 cm from the bottom.

2 Remove the cap of the container.
  ■ Drop a marble into the liquid, and use a timer to measure how long it takes for the marble to pass between the two marks on the side of the container.

  a) Record the time in your table.

3 Put the cap back on the container.
  ■ Invert the container, and measure the time it takes for the marble to pass between the two marks.
  ■ Right the container, and again measure the time for the marble to pass between the two marks.

What property of honey makes it pour more slowly than milk?

b) Record the times in your table.

c) What is the purpose of doing three trials?

d) Calculate the average time for the marble to drop through the liquid.

4 Repeat the investigation using the other three liquids. Make sure the marks are the same distance apart on each container.

e) Record the times in your table.

f) Calculate the average time for each liquid.

g) Why do the marks have to be the same distance apart on each container?

Investigation Questions

1. **a)** In which liquid did the marble take the longest to pass between the two marks?

    b) Is this liquid the most viscous or least viscous? Explain your answer.

2. Rate the liquids from the most viscous to the least viscous.

3. Draw a bar graph to display your data.

Apply

4. Have you ever heard the expression, "Slow as molasses in January"? What do you think it means? Design an investigation to test the viscosity of molasses or corn syrup at different temperatures. With your teacher's approval, carry out your investigation.

Concrete for Construction

TWO PROPERTIES THAT ARE often used in classifying solids are rigidity and strength. Strength is a measure of how well a substance resists stress without breaking. (Stress refers to the internal forces within a material when external forces are applied to it.) The **rigidity** of a substance tells how well it resists being bent.

These properties can be deceptive. Imagine bending a steel bar — it isn't easy. You might assume that steel is very rigid. But what about steel wool? Do you still think that steel is rigid?

Then there's concrete. Have you ever walked across a concrete bridge and felt it move under you as a large truck passed by? You probably thought concrete is rigid too! In fact, virtually every solid can bend to some extent.

In this investigation, you will examine the strength and rigidity of concrete.

Materials

- apron
- empty 1-L milk carton
- scissors
- masking tape
- plastic drop sheet
- concrete mix
- container for mixing cement
- water
- mortar trowel
- wire
- hook
- pail
- bathroom scales
- sand or water

Procedure

Part 1: Building a Concrete Beam

1 Seal the top of the milk carton with masking tape and lay the carton on its side.
- Use scissors to cut away one side of the milk carton.
- Use the cut-away side to make a barrier down the middle of the carton.
- Use masking tape to keep the barrier in place.

2 Mix 2 kg of concrete by adding water to the concrete mix, a little at a time, and mix until all the dry powder has become wet.
- Use the trowel to fill one side of the milk carton with the concrete mix.

3 Repeat step 2 using excess water. The concrete should appear "runny," and when poured into the other half of the milk carton, should have a thin layer of water covering the surface.
- Allow the concrete to cure for two weeks, then carefully peel away the cardboard carton and the divider.

Investigation Questions

1. **a)** Did you record any difference in the mass required to break the two beams?

   b) If you answered yes in (a), can you explain why one beam would break under a different load than the other?

2. **a)** On the basis of your observations, is concrete completely rigid, or does it bend?

   b) If it bends, how could you measure the amount of bend in the concrete as you add sand or water?

Apply

3. Can you suggest a way to make concrete stronger? Would lengthening the beam make it stronger?

Extension

4. Repeat the investigation comparing concrete mixed with just enough water to make the powder wet, and concrete that has been mixed "dry" — some powdered concrete mix is clearly visible when the concrete is poured into the milk carton. Compare the load required to break each beam.

Part 2: Testing Concrete Beams

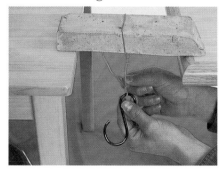

4 Place one of the concrete beams over a gap between two tables.
  ■ Loop a piece of wire around the beam in the middle and attach a hook.
  ■ Determine the mass of an empty pail.
  ■ Suspend the pail from the hook.

5 Gradually add sand or water to the pail until the concrete breaks.
  ■ Determine the mass of the pail and its contents.

a) As you add the sand or water, observe the concrete beam. Does it bend?

b) Record the mass needed to break the concrete beam.

6 Repeat steps 4 and 5 using the other concrete beam.

c) Which beam is stronger, the first beam, or the beam made with excess water?

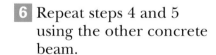

SCIENCE, TECHNOLOGY, AND SOCIETY

Materials and Waste

IMAGINE A SPOON MADE of cardboard. Would you like to eat soup with it? Particular forms of matter are chosen for some applications and not for others because of their distinctive properties. The properties of cardboard make it a poor choice for making spoons. But cardboard does have properties that are useful for packaging.

Continuing Development

Cardboard is a fairly new material. Before cardboard, goods were often packaged in heavy wooden barrels or crates. New materials are being invented every year, and new uses are continually being found for old ones. Some materials can be produced fairly simply. For example, soybeans are grown to provide oil and food. Other materials require complex manufacturing. The custom-designed ceramics used to shield spacecraft re-entering the Earth's atmosphere cannot be grown in fields.

Environmental Considerations

All of this development and progress in materials has come with a cost. In early human history, materials were completely used. For example, when an animal was killed, it provided food. Parts of the animal were made into storage containers. The skin could be used for shelter or clothing. The bones could be converted into tools or weapons. Other parts of the animal were used in religious ceremonies. If a part of the animal could not be used, it would be left for other animals or to decompose.

As goods began to be produced in factories, this pattern changed. Factories use only the parts of a material they need to make their products. Anything that is left over can, in theory, be shipped to other factories, but often it just becomes waste. Consumers generate waste as they discard materials that have become "useless," such as packaging, and broken or worn-out products. As the human population increases, the amount of this waste also increases.

Dealing with Waste

To reduce the amount of waste produced, humans must change their habits. Manufacturers could review their product designs to reduce the potential for waste and, where appropriate, modify the material used. Consumers, through their own actions and choices or through their governments, could force this change.

All of this cardboard was used in packaging. Cardboard is recyclable.

Materials and Manufacturing

ARON GYSEMANS IS an apprentice at Jack Haggis Leather, a shop in Hyde Park, Ontario, specializing in custom riding gear. Using leather that has been treated to resist water and to be easy to clean, Aaron and the rest of the staff make saddles, saddle bags, stirrups, reins, and bridles. All the hardware is made of brass.

"To work with leather requires more than a little patience and an artistic mind," says Aaron. But the patience and skill pay off. "Leather is quite versatile and forgiving," he says, "and, depending on your creativity, the possible applications of leather as a material are endless."

The first step in any project is the selection of the type of leather according to grain, finish, and weight. Patterns for various products can be purchased, or created from scratch. The patterns are laid out and marked on the flesh side of the hide. Cutting must be accurate, to make as little waste as possible. The knives and tools must be razor-sharp to be safe — a dull knife is more likely to slip and result in a severe cut. According to Aaron, "sharpening is an art in itself, and must be practised regularly."

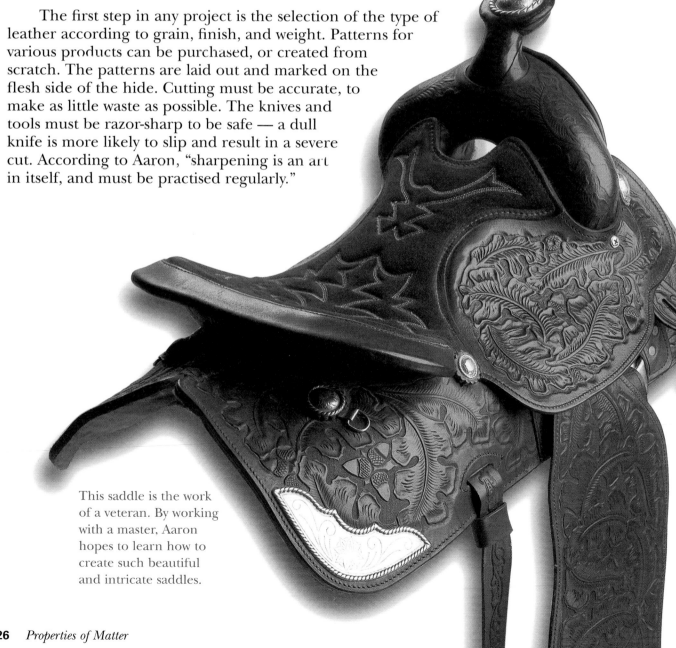

This saddle is the work of a veteran. By working with a master, Aaron hopes to learn how to create such beautiful and intricate saddles.

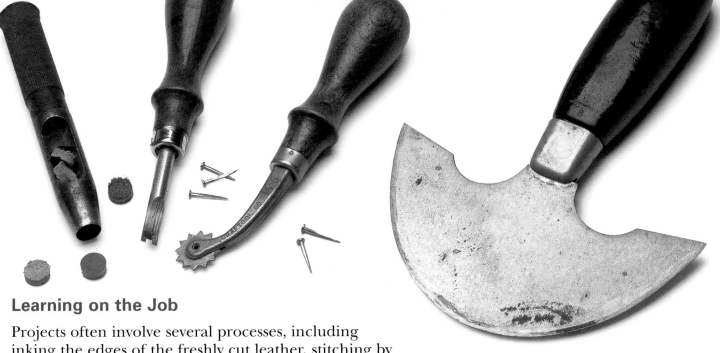

Learning on the Job

Projects often involve several processes, including inking the edges of the freshly cut leather, stitching by machine and by hand, sewing by hand, tooling, and carving.

Aaron is learning from a veteran saddle maker. He has learned how to use a variety of cutting and carving tools to create the intricate shapes and designs of the leather products. He is also learning when and where to use different rivets, staples, and other fastening techniques. From the tools illustrated here, can you identify one that is used for carving? For cutting?

TRY THIS

Working with Leather

How much leather do you need to make a bracelet or necklace? You will need to know the properties of leather, both when it is wet and when it is dry. Based on what you learn, you will have to decide whether your bracelet/necklace can be worn at all times, or whether it will have to be removed when you bathe or take a shower.

- Cut a piece of leather to a length suitable for either a bracelet or necklace. Measure the length.

a) Record your result.

- Place the piece of leather into a bowl of water and allow it to stand for 15–20 min. Remove it and again measure its length.

b) Has any change occurred in its length? Try pulling from either end. Does this result in any change in length?

- Allow the leather to dry overnight. After it has dried, again measure its length and compare with the original.

c) Did the length of the leather change as it dried?

- Based on your observations, choose a suitable length of leather to make a bracelet or necklace.

States of Matter

HOW WOULD YOU GROUP the samples that appear on these pages? Maybe you would put the alcohol, water, and sea water in one group. What properties do the rock, nail, chalk, and nut have in common?

In which group would you put the air and chlorine? Where does the flower fit?

Solids, Liquids, and Gases

Practically every substance that exists can be placed into one of three groups: solids, liquids, or gases. These terms refer to the three states of matter. Clearly, each state has properties very different from the other two. These properties are summarized at right.

SELF CHECK

1. **a)** A loonie coin is sitting on a table. If you carefully picked up the coin and placed it in a glass, would the shape or volume of the coin change?

    b) What state of matter does the coin represent?

    c) What properties do all examples of this state share?

2. If the same amount of water is poured into each of three containers of different shapes, the water will fill each container to a different level. Does each container have a different amount of water in it? Explain.

3. A glass jar is covered with an index card, trapping the air inside. An empty wooden match box is also closed, trapping air inside it.

    a) What is the shape of the air occupying each container?

    b) Is this a property that can be used to distinguish between a liquid and a gas? Explain.

Apply

4. A student argues that table salt is a liquid, because it always takes the shape of the container it is poured into. Do you agree? Why, or why not?

Extension

5. The objects on this page can be grouped as solids, liquids, and gases. But there are other methods of classifying objects. Think about what other properties you might use as organizers, and use them to classify each of the objects.

he States of Matter

olid	Liquid	Gas

he solid pencils do not hange shape when they re put in the container.	All of these containers contain the same volume of liquid.	The volume and shape of the air in the balloon change as the balloon's shape changes.
Shape Definite: has a fixed shape	**Shape** Varies: takes shape of its container	**Shape** Varies: takes shape of its container
Volume Definite: has a fixed volume	**Volume** Definite: has a fixed volume	**Volume** Varies: always fills the entire container

Probing the Earth

A FAMILY HIKING ALONG a creek near Arkona, Ontario, found several fossils embedded in the shale bank along one side of the creek. The fossils were brought to a local museum where the curator was able to tell the family the age of the fossils. Once such a discovery is made, the surrounding area is carefully excavated by hand so that scientists and historians can make inferences about life as it existed in that area. An **inference** is a conclusion that is not based on direct observation.

In much the same way, physicists probe matter for new evidence to help explain the properties and behaviour of matter and to make inferences about what matter is made of.

Materials

- apron
- bolts, nuts, washers, screws, metal shot
- modelling clay or Plasticine
- toothpicks

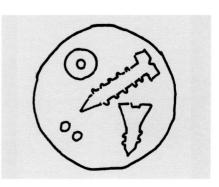

Procedure

1 Bury your hardware in some modelling clay. Roll the clay into a smooth ball so that you cannot see or feel any of the hardware.
- Trade your ball with another group.

2 Use toothpicks to gently probe the clay ball prepared by the other group. Try to find out how many and which kinds of hardware are hidden in the ball.
- Do not pull the ball apart!

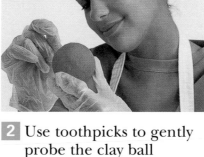

3 Create a map of the clay ball.

a) Draw an outline of the ball in your notebook or journal.

b) Using the results of your probing, draw the pieces of hardware and their locations inside the ball.

4 Carefully pull the clay ball apart.

c) How accurate was your drawing? Did you find all of the pieces with your probe? Did you correctly identify all the pieces?

Investigation Questions

1. As you probed the ball, you used the information you gathered to make inferences about the contents of the ball.

   a) What information would allow you to infer that the ball contained a washer?

   b) What information would allow you to infer that the ball contained a screw?

2. State whether each of the following is an observation or an inference.

   a) The clear, colourless liquid burst into a flame when heat was applied.

   b) The clear, colourless liquid that extinguished the flame must be water.

   c) School is open today but is closed tomorrow, so today must be Friday.

   d) If you leave an iron pot in water, it turns brown.

Extension

3. A mental picture of something you cannot see is often described as a model. Describe an example of a model that you know, and explain what it tells you.

Probing Matter

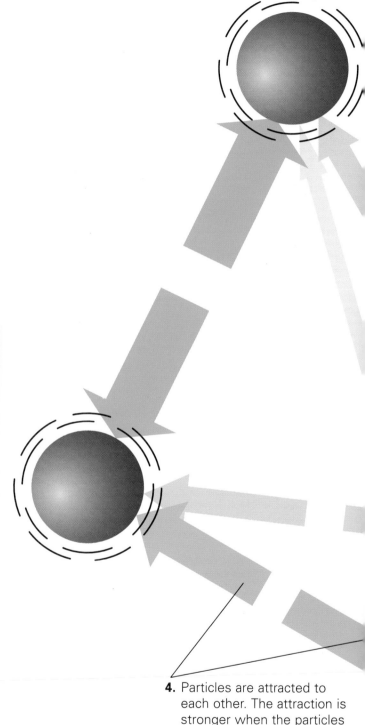

YOU HAVE USED A pointed object to probe a ball of clay to discover the nature and shape of objects inside. Ernest Rutherford, a physicist, discovered a similar probing technique for matter. He fired tiny particles at some matter, and then measured what happened to the particles. Did they bounce? If they did, what angle did they bounce off at? Did they pass through? If they did, did they go straight through, or were they deflected? The answers allowed him to make inferences about the structure of matter.

Scientists have perfected Rutherford's technique so they can probe within the structure of the smallest particles that make up matter, and they have come to some strongly supported inferences about matter.

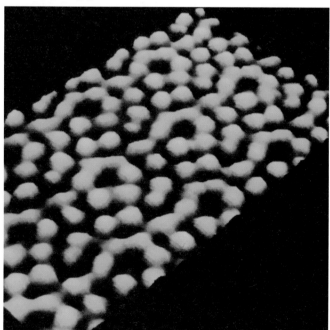

With the new scanning tunneling electron microscope, it is now possible to see the particles that make up matter. This photo shows a very tiny piece of silicon.

4. Particles are attracted to each other. The attraction is stronger when the particles are closer together.

After careful study, scientists have made some important inferences about matter.

1. All matter is made up of extremely tiny particles.

2. There are spaces between the particles.

3. The particles are always moving. The more energy that particles have, the faster they move.

The arrangement of a substance's particles determines whether the substance is a solid, a liquid, or a gas.

Solid

In a solid, the particles are so close together that they can only move back and forth in a small space. Strong attractive forces hold the particles together.

Liquid

In a liquid, the particles are slightly farther apart. They are able to slide past one another because the attractive forces are weaker.

Gas

In a gas, the particles are far apart. The particles can move in any direction because the attractive forces that hold them together are weakest when the particles are far apart.

TRY THIS

Indirect Observations

You can create a model of matter, and use your own probe to explore it. Press four steel marbles randomly into the bottom of an aluminum pie pan to leave an indentation so that the marbles cannot roll around. The steel marbles in the pie plate form a model of matter. Roll a glass marble down a grooved ruler toward the centre of the pie pan, from a variety of positions around the edge. The glass marble is your "probe." Record the path of the glass marble after each roll.

a) One inference that scientists have made is that there is space between particles in matter. Describe an observation you made that would support that inference.

SELF CHECK

1. Copy and complete the following table in your notebook.

	Solid	Liquid	Gas
Type of particle movement	back-and-forth		
Spaces between particles		wider	
Attraction between particles	strong		

Models of Matter

DURING YOUR STUDY OF MATTER and its properties, you have probably discovered that most substances look different from each other, but some, like salt and sugar, are very similar in appearance. What causes such differences and similarities in substances? The answer is in the organization of their particles.

To help them understand particle organization, scientists work with models. In this activity, you will create models of matter using toothpicks to join together marshmallows, which will represent the individual particles of matter.

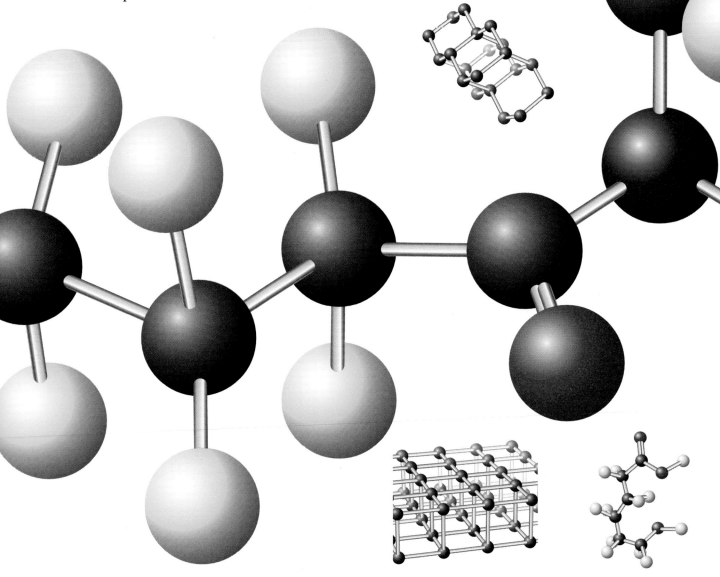

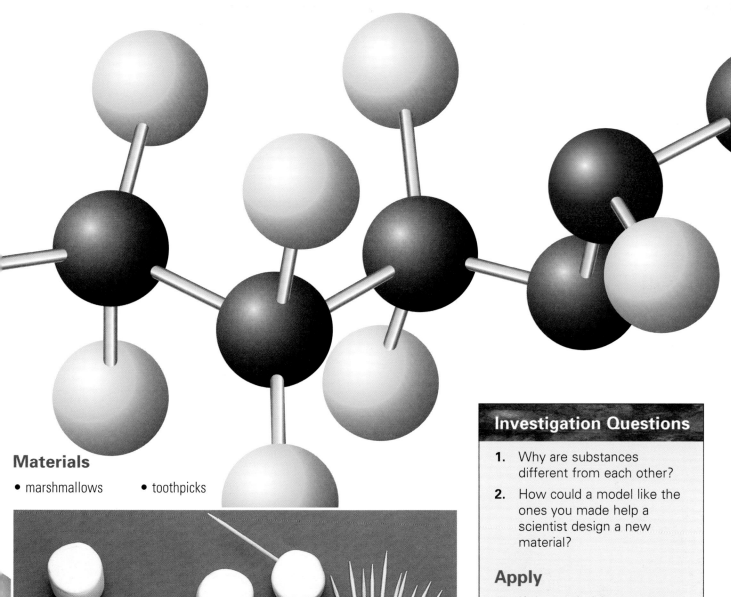

Materials

- marshmallows
- toothpicks

Investigation Questions

1. Why are substances different from each other?

2. How could a model like the ones you made help a scientist design a new material?

Apply

3. If the toothpicks represent the forces of attraction between the marshmallow particles, use your models to describe the difference(s) in the number and location of toothpicks in a solid, a liquid, and a gas.

Procedure

1 Join marshmallows with toothpicks to make a model that you feel represents a solid.

a) What properties of a solid were you able to show in your model?

2 Some solids, such as rubber, stretch easily without breaking. This property is called elasticity. Using the marshmallows and toothpicks, construct a model of a solid that stretches easily, and one that resists stretching.

b) Describe the differences between your two models.

3 Modify your model of a solid to make it represent a liquid.

c) What properties of a liquid does your model show?

4 Modify your model to represent a gas.

d) Does your model show all the properties of a gas? Why, or why not?

Changes in State

I N WINTER, YOU CAN EASILY find water in all three states. Solid water forms snow and ice; liquid water runs under the ice; and there is always some gaseous water (vapour) in the air. Water is a familiar substance that readily changes state. Many other substances go through the same changes, but at different temperatures.

Applying the Particle Model

The particle model that is used to explain the properties of matter can also be used to explain changes of state.

Solid to Liquid

Melting is the change of state from a solid to a liquid.

Liquid to Solid

Freezing or solidification is the change of state from liquid to solid.

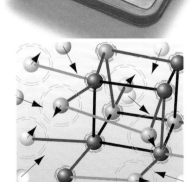

Melting

In a solid, the particles (blue) are held together closely. As heat energy is absorbed, the particles (green) begin to move faster. Some of the particles (yellow) begin to break free. The solid becomes a flowing liquid.

Freezing

When heat energy is removed, the particles move more slowly. The particles come together and form a solid structure.

quid to Gas

porization is the change of state from a liquid to gas.

aporation occurs slowly at the surface of the liquid over a de range of temperatures.

iling occurs at a specific temperature and the gas is formed roughout the liquid.

Vaporization

As heat is added to a liquid, the particles (orange) begin to move faster. Some of the particles (red) break away completely. These particles have large spaces between them — the particles have reached a gaseous state.

as to Liquid

ondensation is the change of state from a gas to a liquid.

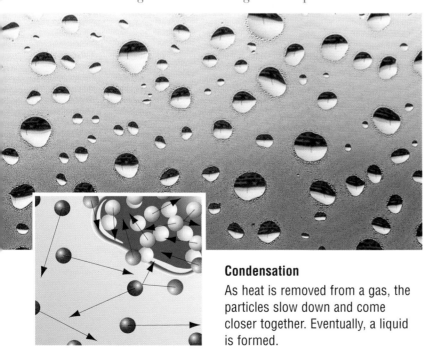

Condensation

As heat is removed from a gas, the particles slow down and come closer together. Eventually, a liquid is formed.

SELF CHECK

1. Copy and complete the following chart in your notebook.

Change of state	From	To	Heat added or removed
Melting	solid		
Freezing or solidification			
Vaporization			
Condensation			

2. What change(s) of state occur when you leave a container of ice cream out on the counter on a warm summer day?

3. Name the changes of state described in each of the following examples.

    a) The water level in an open glass drops over several days.

    b) At a temperature close to 0°C, rain turns to ice when it touches the ground.

    c) Water droplets form on the inside of a window on a cool night.

    d) Dry ice (solid carbon dioxide) forms a "cloud" and then disappears if left out at room temperature.

4. You have seen examples of water coming out of the air and forming condensation on cold objects. How does water get into the air to begin with? What is the process called?

5. When water vapour comes in contact with a cold surface, it condenses. Use the particle model of matter to explain what happens.

Physical Changes

A STREAM OF HOT water erupts into the air and disappears. A frozen popsicle melts in your hand on a hot summer day. Before your very eyes, matter is always changing. Changes like these are called physical changes. In a **physical change,** the properties of a substance may change (for example, ice is different from liquid water), but the substance itself does not change (both the ice and the water are the same substance). If you freeze the melted popsicle, it will become solid again.

In this investigation, you will examine two kinds of change — melting/solidification and dissolving/crystalizing.

Materials

- apron
- safety goggles
- rubber gloves
- electric kettle
- tin can
- retort stand
- clamp
- candle
- ruler
- thermometer
- beaker
- crushed bluestone
- stirring rod
- spoon or scoopula
- thread
- plastic wrap

 CAUTION: Bluestone is toxic if ingested and a strong irritant. Report any spills to your teacher immediately. If bluestone comes in contact with your eyes, rinse your eyes with water for 15 minutes and inform your teacher.

CAUTION: Hot water can scald. Be careful that it does not contact your skin.

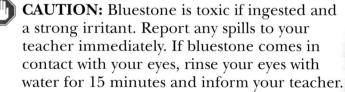

Once the hot water in a geyser explodes out of the earth, where does it go?

Procedure

1 Your teacher will pour boiling water from a kettle into a small can until the can is about one quarter full.

■ Use a ruler to scrape some wax from a candle. Observe the wax carefully.

■ Add the wax to the hot water.

a) Describe the appearance, colour, texture, and odour of the wax before placing it into hot water.

b) Describe what happens to the wax after it is placed in the hot water.

2 Use a thermometer to keep track of the temperature of the water as it cools.

c) Record the temperature at which the wax begins to solidify.

d) Describe the appearance, colour, texture, and odour of the wax once it has solidified.

3 Half fill the beaker with hot water.

■ Slowly add the crushed bluestone to the beaker while stirring. Keep adding bluestone until small amounts start collecting on the bottom of the beaker.

e) Describe the appearance of crushed bluestone.

f) Describe the appearance of the mixture of bluestone and water.

g) Why is it important to stir the water as you add the bluestone?

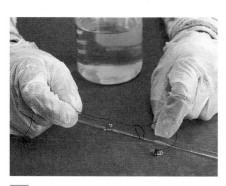

4 Tie one end of a piece of thread around a small crystal of blustone. Tie the other end of the string around a stirring rod.

■ Place the stirring rod across the top of the beaker so that the bluestone crystal is immersed.

5 Cover the top of the beaker with plastic wrap.

■ Place the beaker in an area where it will not be disturbed and observe daily.

h) Record your daily observations.

i) What happens to the liquid in the beaker over the observation time?

Changes in Matter

DOES MATTER CHANGE ONLY its state or form? You have seen wax melt and solidify. Crushed bluestone dissolves in water, but can crystallize again under certain conditions. But what about the change in iron when rust forms on its surface? Plants start out small and grow larger. How can we categorize that change? How are formations of rust and plant growth similar to and different from one another?

Physical Changes

In a physical change, no new substances are created. Changes of state are physical changes. When candle wax melts, it is still wax. Dissolving is also a physical change. When you stirred bluestone into water, the bluestone did not change. It just spread through the water. You showed this when you recrystallized the bluestone.

Melting is a physical change in matter.

Growth and reproduction are biological changes in matter.

Biological Change

Plants grow as they draw water and nutrients from the soil and air and change them into new plant material. The same kind of changes happens in human bodies, as we turn food and water into bone, muscle, and other body tissue.

Changes caused by life processes such as growth, reproduction, eating, and movement are called **biological changes.**

Chemical Changes

In a **chemical change**, a substance changes into another substance with a new set of properties. An example is the chemical change that takes place in the engine of a car: gasoline changes into several gases, including carbon dioxide and water vapour.

One way to determine whether a substance has undergone a chemical change is to try to imagine changing it back into its original form. If this cannot be done, a new, permanent set of properties has been created. A chemical change has occurred. There are some other clues you can use to determine if a change is chemical.

What evidence can you see in this photo that a chemical change has taken place?

Clues That a Chemical Change Has Occurred	
A new colour is evidence of a chemical change.	
Heat or light are sometimes given off in a chemical change.	
In a chemical change, you may see bubbles of gas form.	
Sometimes, a solid material forms in a liquid in a chemical change.	
A chemical change is difficult to reverse.	

SELF CHECK

1. How is a physical change different from a chemical change?

2. Do you think biological changes are physical, chemical, or both? Explain.

Apply

3. List three examples of a biological change.

4. Classify the following changes as physical, chemical, or biological.

   a) Metals exposed to air rust or corrode.

   b) A magnet picks up metallic objects.

   c) Adding yeast to grape juice causes fermentation to begin.

   d) Fish die after chemicals are spilled into a river.

   e) A large diamond is shattered into smaller diamonds for jewellery.

5. Describe each of the following observations as qualitative or quantitative, and identify the change as physical, chemical, or biological.

   a) Sugar burns if sprinkled in a flame.

   b) Green plants need sunlight to grow.

   c) When dropped from a height of 1 m, the ball bounces 70 cm above the floor.

Journal Entry

6. Reflect on the changes you listed in your journal as part of the Getting Started at the beginning of this unit. Organize the changes in your list into physical, chemical, or biological changes. Are there any that do not appear to fit into any group?

Name That Change

Y OU HAVE LEARNED THAT there are three kinds of change: physical, chemical, and biological. It is not always easy to tell the difference between a physical, a chemical, and a biological change—each change must be interpreted with care.

In this investigation, your group will combine samples of familiar matter, and then decide if any changes you observe are physical, chemical, or biological.

Plants are made up of tiny cells. The cells absorb nutrients and use them to produce more cells. As the number of cells grows, the plant grows. Growth is a biological change.

Materials

- safety goggles
- gloves
- apron
- small beakers
- medicine dropper
- baking soda

- vinegar
- water
- milk
- small piece of eggshell
- uncooked spaghetti

- lemon juice
- paper
- candle
- yeast
- molasses
- warm water

Procedure

 a) For each combination, observe the properties of the substances before and after you combine them. Record your observations.

 b) Identify any change you observe as physical, chemical, or biological, based on your observations.

c) If you are not sure of the kind of change, suggest a procedure you might follow that would help you decide. After getting the approval of your teacher, carry out your procedure.

1 Using a medicine dropper:
- Add vinegar to a small sample of baking soda.

- Add water to a small sample of baking soda.

- Add vinegar to a small sample of milk.

- Add vinegar to a small piece of eggshell.

Chemical changes may result in heat or light being released. The explosion of fireworks is a chemical change.

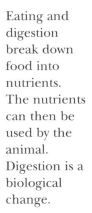

Eating and digestion break down food into nutrients. The nutrients can then be used by the animal. Digestion is a biological change.

On a hot day, the liquid in a thermometer expands. On a cold day, it contracts. This kind of change in volume is a physical change.

Dicing or slicing a carrot doesn't change the materials in the carrot. This is a physical change.

Iron combines with oxygen in the air to produce rust, a new material. Rusting is a chemical change.

2 Dip a piece of uncooked spaghetti into lemon juice.

• Use the spaghetti like a pen to write your initials on a piece of paper.

• Heat the paper gently over a candle flame.

3 Mix yeast and a small amount of warm water.

• Stir some molasses into warm water.

• Pour your yeast mixture into the molasses mixture.

Investigation Questions

1. **a)** List three appearance changes that can occur during a physical change.

   b) Based on your observations, do appearance changes also occur in chemical and biological changes?

   c) Is appearance change a good clue to the type of change a substance undergoes?

2. **a)** What conclusion did you make about the kind of change that takes place when yeast is mixed with a solution of molasses?

   b) What evidence or clues did you observe that would support this conclusion?

   c) Did you follow any additional procedure to help convince you? If so, describe what you did.

Apply

3. Baking soda is a unique substance that has many functions. For example, because it is alkaline (the chemical opposite of acid), it can neutralize acid.

   a) What over-the-counter remedy might contain baking soda as one of its ingredients? Check it out.

   b) Without baking soda, cakes would be flat instead of fluffy. Explain this statement based upon your observations.

4. Refer to your initial observations of the piece of eggshell. Name two properties of eggshell that make it useful to a chicken.

Key Outcomes

Now that you have completed this unit, can you do the following? If not, review the sections listed in brackets.

List and describe a variety of properties that may be used to classify and to identify substances. (1, 2, 3, 5, 6, 7, 9, 10, 11, 13)

Describe a substance using both qualitative and quantitative observations. (5)

Choose materials for various applications based on the properties of the material, cost, and impact of material wastes on the environment. (4, 11)

Explain the meaning of "balance" as it applies to the mass of two objects the same distance on either side of a fixed point. (6)

Manipulate a variety of equipment to measure the mass and volume of different forms of matter. (6, 7, 8)

Consider careers that require knowledge of the properties and uses of several materials. (12)

Observe a variety of substances representing the three states of matter in order to identify characteristics and comparative properties of each state. (13)

Distinguish between direct observations and inference. (14)

Use probing techniques and models of probing techniques in order to develop a particle model for matter. (14, 15)

Create and manipulate models of matter. (16)

Recognize and describe the changes of state that occur among solids, liquids, and gases. (17)

Recognize changes in matter and describe the change as physical, chemical, or biological. (17, 18, 19, 20)

Review Questions

1. An object is placed on the balance pan of an equal-arm balance. Standard masses totalling 8.50 g are added to the opposite pan. What is the mass of the object?

2. Describe at least three physical properties of each of the following:

   a) an apple

   b) a potato chip

   c) a grape-flavoured popsicle

   d) motor oil

3. Two pieces of fruit have the same colour and texture. Name two other properties that might be used to distinguish the two pieces of fruit.

4. Choose one property of matter and draw a diagram to show the arrangement of particles that might give rise to the property.

5. **a)** What is the difference between a quantitative and a qualitative observation?

   b) Give one example of each type of observation.

6. Explain why displacement of water is an indirect measurement of volume.

7. You are given a ball of modelling clay and are told that several objects are embedded in it. You have toothpicks to use as probes. What factor will influence the accuracy of your mental image of the objects in the Plasticine? Explain.

8. Explain how models are useful in science.

9. Describe the equipment you would need and the steps you would take to measure each of the following:

   a) the volume of a ring

   b) the mass of a sample of liquid

   c) the volume of a cement block

   d) the mass of a stone

   e) the volume of a sample of liquid

10. State whether each of the following descriptions represents an observation or an inference.

   a) The clear container in the refrigerator is filled with a yellow liquid.

   b) The yellow liquid in the refrigerator has a tart taste.

   c) When drinking the yellow liquid, one can clearly detect the smell of oranges.

   d) The yellow liquid is orange juice.

   e) The sign in the shop window reads "CLOSED".

   f) If the shop is closed at noon, it means the owner has gone for lunch.

   g) If the shop is closed during business hours, the owner has gone fishing for the day.

11. Draw a diagram to show the arrangement of particles in a solid, a liquid, and a gas.

12. In which state(s) of matter are the following true?

   a) the particles are held firmly in position

   b) the particles are moving the most freely

   c) the particles are closest together

   d) the attractions between particles are the weakest

13. Use the particle model to explain the following changes of state.

    a) Solids melt when heated.

    b) Liquids vaporize when heated.

    c) Gases condense when cooled.

    d) Liquids solidify when cooled

14. In your own words, how could you determine whether a change is physical or chemical?

15. Classify each of the following changes as chemical or physical.

    a) Oxygen gas is liquefied under pressure.

    b) Liquid oxygen is burned as fuel in a rocket.

    c) A liquid, when released from a cylinder, "disappears."

    d) Charcoal is left after wood is burned.

    e) Shaking up a soft drink causes fizzing.

    f) Water boils in a kettle.

    g) Freshly cut fruit turns brown when exposed to air.

    h) A stain in a bathtub is bleached.

16. When you mix sugar in water, the sugar disappears. Explain why this is an example of a physical change rather than a chemical change.

17. Give one example of a physical change and one example of a chemical change that might occur when a meal is prepared.

Problem Solving

18. What is the volume of air in a classroom that is 11.0 m by 9.0 m by 3.0 m?

19. The mass of a dry, empty beaker is 250 g. The mass of the beaker and liquid is 475 g. What is the mass of the liquid?

20. A graduated cylinder contains 40 mL of water. A stone is carefully slipped into the cylinder. The level of the water reaches 57 mL. What is the volume of the stone?

21. The graph shows the mass of a given number of pebbles.

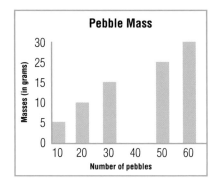

Use the graph to

    a) estimate the number of pebbles in a sample that has a mass of 20 g.

    b) estimate the mass of 110 pebbles.

22. Plot a mass vs volume graph for each of the liquids A and B.

| | **Volume** | | | | |
	0 mL	10 mL	20 mL	30 mL	40 mL
Mass (g) Liquid A	0	10	20	30	40
Mass (g) Liquid B	0	8	16	24	32

Use your graph to find:

    a) the mass of 15 mL of liquid A.

    b) the volume of 35 g of liquid A.

    c) the mass of 25 mL of liquid B.

    d) the volume of 10 g of liquid B.

23. An ice cube is placed on one balance pan of an equal-arm balance. Masses totalling 3.5 g are placed on the opposite pan to level the balance. If the ice cube is allowed to melt, do you expect any change in mass to occur? Explain.

24. A recipe calls for 250 mL of milk, 100 g of ground nuts, and 125 mL of butter. Explain the steps you would take to measure each quantity.

25. Solids are described as having a constant volume. However, most solids expand (increase volume) slightly when heated.

   a) Use the particle theory of matter to explain this observation.

   b) What would happen to a bridge on a hot day if there were no expansion joints?

26. Solidification or freezing is a change of state that releases heat. When a lake freezes at the start of winter, would you expect the temperature over the land near the lake to be warmer or colder than the temperature further inland? Explain.

27. Use the particle model of matter to explain why it is easier to move your hand through air than through water.

28. Every model has its limitations.

   a) Identify one model used in everyday life.

   b) Describe how the model is similar to the real item or idea it represents.

   c) Describe how the model differs from the real item or idea it represents.

29. You are provided with a sample of modelling clay, a piece of string, a graduated cylinder, a balance, and some water. Use these materials to prove that the shape of the clay can be changed without changing the mass and volume of the clay.

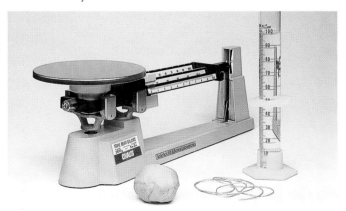

30. A student is given a sealed metal can without a label. The student shakes the can, and, because the contents slosh around inside, concludes that the can contains water. Knowing that water freezes at 0°C, the student places that can in a freezer at 0°C and finds that the contents solidify.

   a) Can the student be certain that the can contains water?

   b) Is this a description of a model? Explain.

31. In an experiment using different combinations of substances, Larry uses the following evidence to justify his choices of chemical changes. Are they valid? Explain.

   a) "When I opened a can of cola, it fizzed. This showed that a chemical change had occurred."

   b) "Heat and light are given off by a light bulb. A chemical change is taking place in the light bulb."

   c) "When I sawed through the piece of wood, smoke came up around the power saw blade, and the sawdust appeared blackened around the edges. Because the sawdust appeared different from the wood it came from, a chemical change occurred."

Projects for Investigation

32. Food cooks rapidly in a microwave oven. Microwaves put energy into the water particles inside the food. Research how microwaves work and use the particle model to explain why microwaves cook food so quickly.

33. A car's fuel pump is designed to pump fuel in its liquid form. In winter, water vapour in the gas tank can condense and even freeze. What effect is this likely to have on the car? In summer, at high temperatures, the fuel may vaporize. What effect is this likely to have on the operation of the car?

Glossary

B

boiling: the change of state from a liquid to a gas; occurs at a specific temperature and the gas is formed throughout the liquid (p. 37)

C

chemical change: a change in which a substance is changed into another substance with a new, permanent set of properties (p. 41)

clarity: a property describing how well a substance transmits light; ranges from transparent to opaque (p. 9)

colour: a property that describes which kinds of light a substance reflects (p. 8)

conductivity: a property describing how easily electricity flows through a substance; substances range from being good conductors to insulators (p. 9)

condensation: the change of state from a gas to a liquid (p. 37)

D

ductility: a property that describes how easy it is to pull a substance into a new, permanent shape (p. 9)

E

elasticity: a property that describes how well a substance snaps back to its original shape after it is stretched (p. 8)

evaporation: the change of state from a liquid to a gas; occurs slowly at the surface of the liquid over a wide range of temperatures (p. 37)

F

freezing (or solidification): the change of state from liquid to solid (p. 36)

function (or application): the way in which a material is used (p. 10)

H

hardness: a property that describes the resistance of a substance to scratching (p. 8)

I

inference: a conclusion that does not come from direct observation (p. 30)

K

kilogram: the basic SI unit for measuring mass (p. 12)

L

litre: the basic SI unit for measuring volume (p. 12)

lustre: a property describing the way a substance reflects light; how shiny a substance is (p. 8)

M

malleability: a property describing how a solid responds to hammering; substances range from being malleable to brittle (p. 9)

mass: the measure of the amount of matter in a substance (p. 12)

matter: anything that has mass and occupies space (p. 4)

melting: the change of state from a solid to a liquid (p. 36)

P

physical change: a change in which the properties of a substance may change, but the substance itself does not (p. 38)

properties: the characteristics, or attributes, of a substance (p. 6)

Q

qualitative observation: an observation made using the senses, but using no measurements (p. 12)

quantitative observation: an observation in which a measurement is made (p. 12)

R

rigidity: a property that describes the resistance of a substance to bending (p. 22)

S

solubility: a property describing how well a substance mixes with another substance (p. 8)

state: a property describing whether a substance is a gas, a liquid, or a solid (p. 8)

strength: a property describing how much stress a substance can take before breaking (p. 8)

T

texture: a property describing how the surface of a substance feels (p. 6)

V

vaporization: the change of state from a liquid to a gas (p. 37)

viscosity: a property that describes the way liquids pour (p. 8)

volume: the measure of the amount of space occupied by an object, or the hollow space inside the object (p. 12)